Bruce Majors has published poems in *Pirene's Fountain, Ontologica, Wordgathering, Arts and Letters, Pinesong, The Distillery, River Poets Journal, Number One*, and other fine literary journals. His collection, *The Fields of Owl Roost*, was named finalist in the 2005 Indie Excellence Book Awards. Two chapbooks, *Last Flight of Angels* and *Small Patches of Light*, were published in 2013 and 2015, respectively, by Finishing Line Press. He co-edited an anthology, *Southern Light: Twelve Contemporary Southern Poets*. Mr. Majors is a member of the Chattanooga Writers Guild.

What I Know About Light

Poems by
Bruce Majors

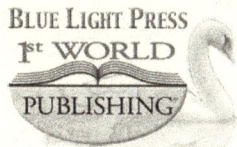

BLUE LIGHT PRESS
1st WORLD
PUBLISHING

San Francisco | Fairfield | Delhi

What I Know About Light

Bruce Majors

ISBN: 978-1-4218-3663-8

Library of Congress Control Number: 2020940876

1ST WORLD LIBRARY
PO Box 2211
Fairfield, Iowa 52556
www.1stworldpublishing.com

BLUE LIGHT PRESS
www.bluelightpress.com
Email: bluelightpress@aol.com

I would like to thank Donald Buttram for using his skills with a computer and formatting and reviewing this document.

I would also like to thank Patricia Majors for her expert work in the editing and layout of this book.

And special thanks to Cathy Ann Kodra for her expert review and edit of the book.

My appreciation to the following journals and one anthology for publishing my poems:

Abyss & Apex: "The Black Unicorn," "Hall of Mirrors"

Anthology of Southern Literature: "Prozac Dream"

Clapboard House: "Flying like Angels," "Passing by Pleasant Hill Baptist Church at Dusk," "Message of Snow," "Quietness After the Noise"

GFT Press: ". . . From Niagara Village," "Moments of Felicity"

Howl Magazine: : "Dark Rooms," "Suspended by Air"

Inflate Magazine: "Shooting Bottles in the Tennessee River"

Into the Void Magazine: "Breakfast"

Number One Magazine: "Valleys of the Moon," "Heat Lightning," "Soldier," "At the Coffee Shop," "Love Song," "Night Watch," "Void"

Pirene's Fountain: "Solitary Places"

Rosette Maleficarum: "Night Visitors"

The Distillery: "About Snow," "Winter Sun"

TABLE OF CONTENT

Chasing Starlight

Prayer of Leaves

A Little Psalm

What I Know About Light

MOMENTS OF FELICITY

Late evening creeps into the barn
through cracks in weathered boards,
spills onto mangers a burnt-orange
reflection of dreams I had as a boy,
climbs the pinioned walls
to soak hayloft and hay bales
with remnants of those dreams.

Mice play in feed bins, cajole
the cat, shadows big as beagles.

The fading light searches tack room.
A small breeze rises near the lake,
lifting a few leaves in unison.
The sun pauses listlessly,
yawns an orange glow,
then slips over Walden's Ridge.
I hear the mice and the cat, her low growls.
Content with the gloaming, the horses shuffle
in their stalls. Owl tremolos signaling
the evening hunt. Stillness of the meadow
works its way into the fabric of night.

Far off, the world invades: jet contrail,
car horn. In broken mood, I leave
my rambling thoughts to mice and cat.
The moments of felicity I keep myself
for another time.

. . . From Niagara

Driving back from the village, from dreams,
past cherry orchards and gardens
(we found Niagara cherries in season),
past white B&Bs where famous people
stayed,
past street crones pushing carts of rags,
past old men in sidewalk bars nursing beers,
telling the prophesy of old age,
the reverie of broken sunlight danced
diamonds on water.

Thermals carry an osprey.
The willow waves its many arms.

Gulls, like splotches of white paint,
careen over the mist. The great water,
deafening, pushes its way into the
violent canyon below,
battering the rocks with myths and legends.

Heat Lightning

I lowered the anchor over the side and watched
as the splayed, cast iron behemoth plundered
through green light to the bottom. Waves lapped
boat ribs, making a drowsy metallic thud.

Forked-tongued, pink lightning struck the western night sky,
threatening bad weather.

Naw, it's just heat lightning, Tom graveled.
Won't bother us.

I thought of electric fences and how lightning coursed
along the wire once, killing a man not ten feet from me.

I thought of electric fences and how lightning coursed
along the wire once, killing a man not ten feet from me.

I thought of my own un-holiness and how
the fires do not purge. I thought of a thousand ways to die.

The heat-cracked night pressed down.
The water, the only certainty. I exist somewhere
between God and my understanding of God.

Rainy Day, Imaginary Lover

The tilting rain came fast and hard.
Racing for the barn, too late.
Both soaked in mild October.
You said the rain would cleanse our souls.

The light inside the barn changed itself
in dusty shadows, how it filtered
through sullen clouds to streak the hallway
with luminescence like
the deluge outside.
How sensual the droplets,
silver like dew, that
somehow broke apart
in small blue spatters
and flecked your face.

The quiet patter on the tin roof evoked
an embrace, a kiss, a cloister of passion.
How we locked and separated so easily.
How the magic closed around us.
Imaginary lovers in a day of rain.

AT THE COFFEE SHOP

They gather each morning around
the table, to discuss
nothing in particular, a quartet of old men
at the Coffee Shop.

There's so much sadness in the world.

With wrinkles and emaciated smiles,
their eyes fall on the loneliest
corners in the room.

Age does not satisfy as we once thought.
With it comes the knowledge
things will not change. We are
not better for having experienced the
pains of life.

The conversation is sparse on this
cool October morning. As they
sip hot coffee or tea, one or two speak
in low, monotonous voices. Thought
I heard him say cancer, but maybe
he said censor.

Out on the street, fog had not lifted.
Red lights, barely visible.
Somewhere in the din of invisibility,
a siren screamed, and then another.
Probably been a wreck over on the bypass,
                    one old man said.

My Father's Prayer on Sawyer's Hill at the Church of God Tabernacle When Revival Came to Town

The preacher railed and pointed to Heaven,
clouds of holy words spewed from his mouth.
His tongue fluttered and wailed,
many were slain in the Spirit,
others lifted arms and shouted.

Some souls even touched the serpent,
lifted faith to a high fist of venom.
He took us over the edge of fire and back.
Finally, his shirt-soaked sermon finished,
he wiped righteous sweat with white handkerchiefs,
sins washed away.

I was seven years old and
I reckoned that was about as close to hell
as I had been.

And when that anointed saint prayed,
folks fell on hands and knees
before the altar. Mumbled.
Prayers offered up a garbled noise into
moon-silvered night . . .

Dad didn't go. I nudged, he wouldn't go.

He should be there with the others,
praying for us . . . or himself. I whispered.

God would surely dampen the flames I felt
if Dad would only go . . .

He stared an angry *Stop!* at me,
but the voice in my head spoke in tongues
I didn't understand.

I kept urging—

With malice, Dad went up to face God. He knelt.
Clasped head in hands. Voice like thunder,
he yelled and yelled . . . still the flames burned
around my feet.

Dad was doing something wrong.

That night we were not changed.
Whatever Dad pleaded, God saw fit not to answer.

WILD THINGS

Out in the fields corn is waist high.
The old tillage tool lies broken with
age. In the grove beyond the pond,
deer lie in the cool shade waiting
for me to leave. Watching my every
movement, measuring my intent,
they don't know I wish them no
harm. Today is my peaceful day.
I could have got them all, oh, all six
lying in the grove, but today is not
for hurting. Today is not for killing
though I could have killed them all.

Something spooked one or two, and I watched
as they made high, arching leaps,
retreating to the dark woods at the end
of the corn. Beautiful, those high, graceful
arcs, leaping through pure air in slow motion,
floating into nothing but memories.

Turning away, I spot an owl on a tree limb,
rudely staring without blinking. Not as
leery as the deer, he grips his limb
never taking the large, all-seeing eyes from
me, nor I him. Later I saw that same owl
holding a field mouse with one claw and
tearing flesh with his razor beak . . . *Nothing lasts*,
I thought, *we all must die.*

DEATH SONG

A great convocation of leaves shakes loose, scurries across the porch,
they have escaped murder for one more day.

Running for their lives, a cluster of souls
sweeps along the railroad trailing spirits of tall shadows,
rises up into the air above the river.

In the stony silence between heart beats,
two boys break loose. One cries out,
squatting beside a small pool where the stream
lies still and silent, calls to his mother: Do you love me?

The other, more callous one, turns into
the valley of a covert leaf.

The yard is full of escaping animals;
shots ring out, and some of the animals fall down
Noxious curses from shadow figures pronounce the law.
Burned in unholy ovens. No one remembers they were here.

The young son cries out to his mother, Do you love me?
The object lies naked on a table.
There is no mother's voice, no love, only the cold wind
through the open window.

VALLEYS OF THE MOON

$E=mc^2$
    —*Albert Einstein, Visionary*

He needed to see the black disk,
study the golden edges of light slipping out
and what stars might appear.

He needed to know if angels live
there guiding the destiny of brilliant men,
spinning theories for curious men to wonder.

At the place of honored souls,
he needed the illusive prize,
the first to garner the equations,

new thinking, transcendent and bold,
what would anneal science in a modern world,
break the backs of skeptics.

A stoop-shouldered crane
sits on my dock, prehistoric fisherman waiting
for an opportunity in murky water,

losing himself in the gray overcast, merging
elements, not at all unlike God particles
buried within some foggy recess

of Einstein's math. The man could have lost it,
never been completely sure he found it.
Someone would have, though. Crunched

the data and proved the theory. We might have
remained naïve forever, were it not
for those devil angels in the valleys of the moon.

What I Know About Light

Light refracts in a prism, bends
its way through space, dispelling darkness,
even darkness gathered around our bodies.
We float there like amber medallions,
flecks of glowing embers.

The milkmaid's path, where she danced,
spilling the light of stars,
is our playground. A handful of brightness,
our medals to bargain with.
Let us tempt angels, we say, *let us fly
through halls of heavenly illumination.*

Neither dark nor light, we tunnel
our way through the ambivalent void
and exist only as something shining
in the universe, like a quarter in a man's pocket.
Small light in a vast darkness.

HALL OF MIRRORS

There is no pain, you are receding
a distant ship, smoke on the horizon
                    —Pink Floyd

Walking down the narrow hall, mirrors set
so that it is possible to walk into eternity,
getting smaller and smaller till I do not exist.
The char of life compels me to
this life-maze of uncertain identities.

In side mirrors, odd shapes make grotesque
images, how we actually appear without
covers of falseness. Nothing looks the same as before.
I harbor the thought that none of this is real,
that I am only a dream of some sleeper's indulgence,
a germ of sleep's theater. Am I dreamer or dream?
The taciturn answer I fear is "neither," walking
and walking forever with nothing before and nothing after.

Attempting to cast my fear aside, I scream I am alive,
the long echo resounding through the mirrors
with no answer. No one is there. Mirrors deepen.
I hold my place, unsure of footing. A small crack at first,
rising to a deafening crash, then the calamity of
shattering complexity. Sleepers awaken, unaware
of the night's passing muse. I lie eternally broken,
a thousand shards of glass, my dream of life thus ending.

A Cloud of Bees

Here in this presence of the past,
content to do their work,
a sundown of bees
swarms a fencepost in the orchard.

Soon they'll need a hive.

Dancing the secret latitudes and longitudes,
the way to the honey pots,
the little circular flights come and go,
repeating ancient rituals,
keeping nature's sweet promise.

The bees never left what they knew,
never took to the world of loss and regret.

Clover meadow, blackberry, sourwood,
their humming rhapsodies greet the blossoms
of spring, heavy yellow legs dusting
anther and pistil, blessing the fruit of
life in this sacred season.

Walking the fields, wind delivers
the droning thrum to my ears, a song
ferried through the centuries
on the backs of new leaves.

Broken Strand

BROKEN STRAND

Out across the lake bed, stumps
appear like bronze castings in
winter's early morning light. Fog
presses down low, curling itself into
the village heart. Far distant crows,
messaging.

Lights in little kitchens come on
late, as if the women there had said:
Wait until this heaviness passes.
Men in stables mend worn leather,
whatever will be needed for spring
plowing.

Farther out on the point, winter water recedes.
Barely outlined, cranes splinter the marsh
as they land.
Blue herons search the edges for minnows,
their stabbing heads like spears slashing
the shallows.

The quietness of fog
vexes me.

Far off, the sound of sandhills trumpeting calls
like angels searching for a hidden Heaven.

How will the Christ in them ever find us here
silent, on this broken strand?

LAST FLIGHT OF ANGELS

Sleep drifted away like morning fog.
I dragged myself to the kitchen and drank coffee.

The birds' rattling sounds told me
they were about to leave, heading north.

It's time to go, they seemed to say, *it's time*.

From the back porch, I wrestled goodbyes,
felt saddened beneath their convoluted circling,
as if reciprocating my farewell.

Wave after wave, they sailed along the narrow
strand of water, out of sight, the last flight
of angels.

The thundering silence heavy in air.

Nothing left but the empty lake bed and,
in the woodlot beyond, the bright,
black coven of crows.

A Certain Chill

I think it's knowing there is
an end of it all, or the fact
that mortality meets me
face to face each day.

The future exists only in a series
of backward glances, mostly dim
memories of dreams that were never
fully realized.

It is autumn. Early frost, judging
from the caterpillars.
There is a certain chill in the
changing air and in my hollowness.

A young man in a red coat, an old
man in a wool sweater. Recollections
that don't fit into either context.
And still, there's the end of it all.

We Are One

Docs want to look at my brain,
crack open my head and peer inside.
It makes a sound when I think.

Thoughts pour out as yellow dust,
wooden rattles, bamboo wind chimes,
and nightmares.

Together, like cooling lava. Riven,
one side loves music, the other, pain.
We sleep together in each other's dream.

Like Janus faces, a damask rose,
the other, damask steel.

MEDITATION IN COLD AIR

I watched the birds for a while.
Sitting by the fireplace, I could
see their erratic flight gaining
altitude toward the cut-
over silage fields by the river.

The cold doesn't seem to bother
as they descend into
the new feeding grounds, flight
after flight overpowering frigid air.

High winds make air feel like a cold
butcher knife. It cuts my skin even
here on the ground in the house.
The hearty birds don't seem to notice;
they seldom think about their lives.

An owl rises from the dark field
clutching a young rabbit.

BREAKFAST

I was thinking about
this morning
at breakfast, when

you said you didn't
really care anymore,
how fragile the

plates were and
how delicate the
tiny flowers

around the borders,
when you said
you thought we

needed to be apart, how
the tablecloth had
a spot and how it

didn't seem to fit,
how the room slid
to one side.

THE MEETING

They meet each day in the hall.
Nothing more.
She has a quiet beauty,
a presence. Dark eyes.

Secretly he loves her though
he cannot say it. They
live in different worlds.

Today his expression,
as they pause to say hello, pinched,
pale, almost choked.

What, she said? Is something
wrong?

Yes, he said. Everything.

Chasing Starlight

CHASING STARLIGHT

There you are in a cloud in my dream.
How could it be that I have missed you?
So often I've felt something, a sensation
or presence, but I never reckoned anything
like this.

How many times have I wanted to turn you on
and was afraid? I've wanted to touch you
outside the dream, but the dream is absolute.

I see your shadow just as I turn, an elusive sprite
dancing across the empty meadows of my mind,
an enigma that won't go away. Just as I reach,
you glimmer out of sight.

How can I capture your spirit, hold starlight in my hand?

Night Scene: An Elegy

—ffor Bruce Majors, Sr.

Night, black wolf stalking red eyes
of the horizon, must be little cities there.

He roams, pressing wet muzzle
against window panes where patients hide
and against window panes of the tall
building where pain hides.

Blinking lights surround beds
and lab coats twirl needles,
death so close no one breathes.

Old women turn their heads and cry.

Repeatedly the sandman comes with noxious sleep.
In white jacket and surgical mask,
he bears vague predictions.

Is it not enough? I cried.
Dear God, is it not enough?

HEAVY BREATH

For weeks I have been unable to function as an adult,
shadows of winter hiding behind the barn.

I walked the knobs to Swafford pond in the lower hollow.
There was nothing there for me.

Small lights blink along Walden Ridge to the west
as the sun draws its last heavy breath. I am left alone

with night bugs, barn owl, and the heavy oak
whose acorns have already begun to drop.

CREATION

Silken weave,
spun with morning dew,
burns cool
in first sun,
hung like diamonds
around the stem of royalty.

Tiny spider,
do you know
what treasure you possess?

Nothing less
than the artistry
of God.

In My Garden Briers Have Replaced the Sun

In my garden of imagination
filled with heartaches and tombstones,
rows of peas and corn and the soil,
my hands in the soil.

All winter the wild roses
grew in abundance, my life of thorns.

The dark soil turned over like a rushing waterfall
exposing the dark underside.

Hands felt the coolness of dirt
moist and deep brown,
rich with the stuff of life.

The warm earth splits the seed pod,
and the tuber seeks new light.

THE LAST DAY OF HISTORY

Not with a bang but a whimper.
            —T.S. Elliot

I see in the sky troubling signs unfolding,
the universe coming apart in cascading waterfall of fire.
The day comes on wings of wind singing:
            what is the mind of war, where is light? Where?

Not completely light or completely dark, but the distressing
gray in between.

Suddenly the sun explodes in a cataclysmic spectacle,
a giant sparkler on 4th of July. We count collateral damage.
There is none. The soldiers are dead.

THE EXACT LOCATION OF ETERNITY

No one knows the exact location of eternity,
although it seems to be somewhere
between Cleveland and Memphis.

The path I choose leads through the heart of the woodland,
winding through low branches and briers,
skirting a slew backed up from the Tennessee River.
This could be eternity or Heaven
or the difference between the two.
I move cautiously, anticipating a shack or hermit's cabin
nestled in some small glade hidden from the world of men
or maybe a family of little people
who live among the roots of a hollow oak.

The pathway is enchanting.
My thoughts leave reasonableness behind,
wander effortlessly through the strange,
magic land with chocolate bunnies
and blue robin's eggs. Ribbons and bobbins . . .
flowers that sing.

In the Deep Forest Glade

The pungent smell of moss and fern.
The deep glade far in the forest.
No place for strangers or scoffers.
No post office or zip code, main street covered with crabapple trees.
Animals inhabit this garden, bears and coyotes, squirrels and rabbits,
badgers, owls, an abundance of birds, especially winter Jays.
A special harmony transforms, lifts up, transcends . . .
Trillium blooms in the deep glade in solitude of summer—
I have often walked here by moonlight and midday sun—
in that same solitude.

A Man of Fields

The old man bent with years,
not the type bothered with time,
seemed ageless as the mighty oaks.
A man of fields and woods with muscle
and nerve. Furrowed land and crops.

183 acres his kingdom. Ridge land
hard as he was. His mules, Jude and Kate,
broke the red-clay rocky-soil hillside turner deep.
They knew Irish temper and plowed straight.

Better men tipped their hats when he approached.
When he spoke, they listened.

Today Poppa looks old, eyes once filled with fire,
smoky gray. Doesn't know my name.
Even giants of the land are mortal.

Prayer of Leaves

ANGUISH

Already the birds are back. That means winter
bearing down with no hope of being saved.

Circling the dry lake bed behind my house,
set their wings, glide down the muddy strip,
landing gracefully on the dry lake bed.

Already my soul stiffens knowing the difficulties
winter brings. Shorter days with less sun. Sun that tilts
away from us, leaving prayer stranded in slanting light.

The chilled air announces the changing of light,
O that dreaded metamorphosis.
Already my bones ache from the cold.

Tall pines whisper Gregorian-like tunes.
Arching through piercing air, searching winter cornfields,
the cranes don't seem to notice loneliness mounting in my life.

Does the end come like a thief in the night?
Is my soul ready for winter?
Loud trumpeting cries overhead seem to say
they don't care.

WHEN LOUIS SLOTIN BEGAN TO DIE

He tickled the dragon's tail.

At exactly twenty minutes past three
Louis Slotin began to die,

the American people didn't know,

the blue air too much
around his hand and
around his head.
Like any other man would, he began to die.

He wore sharp-toed boots,
pant legs stuffed in, short
and feisty, ran a
rockin' little lab, swinging scientific,
a place to tickle the dragon's tail, to
tempt unlimited madness.

In that desert canyon, in that lab
where generals' dreams were made,
the silver hemispheres came together
too quickly: they rattled and banged.
The crackle, like an old radio,
dead static. Dead silence. Dead
scientific detachment. He made a map
of his death . . . plotted where the onlookers
stood and their dosages . . .

Only he began to die.

The generals gave their orders as usual,
the barbed wire lay in coils as usual,
Enrico Fermi worried as usual,
Oppenheimer played his game of chess as usual,
people of the desert didn't know as usual,
ladies of the night as usual,
bus stopped at the general store as usual,
soldiers marched,
earth moved on,
they didn't know, as usual. But

at exactly twenty minutes past three
Louis Slotin began to die.

The Indians who kept the houses didn't know.
The Doctors didn't know.

Wind like animal-howls
screamed through canyons
in the desert when it happened.
The Navajo bareback on his horse
listened. Laboratory screams.
Canyon sided, government issued screams
near Los Alamos.

The purple tumble-weeded sky
didn't know.

At exactly twenty minutes past three
Louis Slotin began to die.

When the alarms went off, no one looked.
When odd shapes appeared behind the fence,
they didn't notice.
Those strange games took away surprise;
no one was amazed.
Lives lived side by side,
like drunks who couldn't remember.
Hot spots didn't matter.
Plutonium waste didn't matter.
They would have carried on even if
the desert turned to ashes.

The desert dwellers didn't know.
The Indians on the reservation didn't know.

Air turned blue, intense heat, sour taste.
In that split second, atoms split
like a criticality of Christmas tree lights
and
at exactly twenty minutes past three
Louis Slotin began to turn to ashes.

He thought of Jenny's smile,
the white stockings,
her eyes. His father's voice, the
tension between them.
His brother, if he had
gone to fight with his
brother . . . The perception
of that blue flash. That deadly crackle.

Note: Louis Slotin died nine days after receiving a massive dose of radiation at a government lab near Los Alamos, NM. He was working on the Manhattan Project when a criticality event occurred. Seven others in the room survived, although three of the seven died some years later of blood-related disease attributable to exposure from that same radiation.

PRAYER OF LEAVES

The ground weeps prayer of brown leaves,
dry scratching voices, prayer of worried claims.

Prayer as gray as January in this place of ghosts
of earlier, sweeter Januaries. It *was* voices . . .
or wind down the hollow of pines growling my name,
calling me to this melancholy life.

It may have been wind?
Or imagination so finely honed
as to make the sound of Heaven
clamoring in my name.

Parched, yellow, desperate prayer,
floundering supplication
hoping the Christ is there, listening.

I have become a pillar of salt

Struggling for word, my failing prayer.

O they are not forgiven

I kneel, I stand, mumble incessantly,
follow the prayer as it goes up the hill of God,
before me, up to Zion or Sinai,
out of the wilderness or deeper into . . .

Quietness for Someone
Who Has Been in the Noise

(1)

Below the rim of ridges
in the fields of owl roost,
two young owls play with a rabbit.
The rabbit squeals.
Blood squirts from his side.
The owls are delirious.

I am learning
to see the cruel winter
as a quiet, red rose.

(2)

An acorn drops into a small pond.
Ringlets scatter until tension
shakes the pond's surface.

I am stricken with the fragileness
of clouds.
Insects shimmer in delicate light.

(3)

I walked into the fields
for the way they looked today.
This place holds my soul
in a wooden box
filled with tall oaks.
Slowly evening turns gold
and settles in a haze
over the fields.
If I stand still and listen,
I can hear the advancing shadow of trees
whisper my name.

(4)

Fresh rain
wets my face and hair.
Water drips from every leaf.
Mists rise up from the ground.
When I step into the air,
wind finds me.

I Did Not See You Leave

—Elegy for Roy Frazier

You slip into your silence, rattles choking
life into another world. A wink as light came in,
a realm of intriguing possibilities, an irrevocable
freedom to become another entity on some other pure plane.

I didn't see you leave, only a worn body no longer
needed, but I did not see the soul—
and I looked—rise up, hover over son or wife, then, like air

that shakes one or two leaves, mingle with eternity.
Fixed, translucent eyes went dim, hollow mouth
drooling death-venom, swollen body

needing rest only earth can give. But I didn't see
you leave. Possibly only angels saw, and stars.
Heaven may have shouted, the white doors flung

open with sounds of thunder and heralding trumpets—
but all mortal eyes could see were tears of grief.
Death can be measured in that way.

MUSINGS

The bush hog roils the field,
churns tall grass and occasionally
a rabbit's nest or a young fawn
blown out the side.

No one knows how life will play out;
it may be just a game of chance,
a poker hand, a roll of dice.

Wind drifts leaves onto the roof
of my cabin, acorns drop, plunk
with a metallic thud, quickly
swallowed up by nature's hunger
to replenish. Doves whistle the air,
searching for safe haven.

Fall yellows pumpkins, the moon
overtakes reddened skies.
Seasons turn like some great axle of
unknown spaces, ratcheting time forward,
the gray matter of pulsing neutron
stars.

High up in the ridge, the owl calls
to his lonely god. We live on as usual.

Water molds my dock, the odor
of rotting milfoil stagnates
the afternoon. A snake makes its way
across the slew, and I am stricken with joy.
How wonderfully separate we are.

The hawk takes his prize from the field.
I have searched the hills and woodland
for what I believed was there.
No one knows the days ahead, good or bad.
I lie, transparent, in the cave of fields.

HIGHWAY 27 SOUTH OF SPRING CITY

Sun drifts in red clouds toward night.
First stars come out.

Mosaic of muscle cars gather
on an abandoned gas station lot,
in this broken down town
on East Tennessee 27.

Outside their cars, boys in ball caps
in groups of three and four, talking,
southern expletives buzzing.
Big block engines, four wheel drives that
can do anything, and girls

that will do anything.

This is the heart of summer.

Conversations are more humid, less complicated,
all about oil filters, tractors,
race-car drivers.

Night falls beneath the stars.

I hear their diminished voices,
uncertain laughter until only a low roar remains
of what might still be laughter
or lingering cries as I slowly pass.
Sometimes I think there may be more—fears, or unspoken dreams
in those school-boy faces.

The road, chunks of missing pavement,
rattles along with my old Ford south of town.

I'm thinking how I would like
to be like them . . .

always half a step away
half-dark and half-light,
like that time of evening

when the first stars come out,
too big for words.

IMAGINARY LOVER

Once in Chicago I could have,
but I didn't do it.

You left the same.

Now lonely as a broken doll,
wanting to breathe but no air.

The scent of you everywhere,
the dress you left,
bath powder,
the window seat where
you curled when it rained.

I walk the house at night
searching for you,
your image, back-lit, glowing,
filters light into my waking dream,

the bed, empty on one side,
crazy on the other.

STRING QUARTET

The music coming from her window
is chamber music, a Janacek piece,
a string quartet.

Janacek is perfect for her,
the perfection of sound, inadvertent mystery
of brown eyes wide and dark.

I imagine her smooth body a coffin of air,

clear, invisible river of sound,
caressing her,
pressing a perfect mold of her
to keep forever in music of glass,
her loving me forever,
violating all I know of love and art.

A small riffle of wind separates
and she is gone in a thousand sparkles of light
like moonlight spackled on ruffled water,
a glimmer of motion dimpled apart,
teasing, like the dragon fly teases a toad.
Laughing herself into the invisible
mid-world below,
her music fills the night, a curling waterfall . . .
Finds me in blue loneliness of night's
summer sidewalk
below her window, dreaming.

Snow Country

The snow,
      even the air, is blue
      in this tundra-like place.

A silver fox darts into a snowbank,
chasing a mouse,

hidden

somewhere deep in the sleeping grass.

Wind scuffs a hillside,
whirls a cloud of snow at the lava sun,
pales into a red glint.

SUSPENDED BY AIR

Holding this rail
suspended by air,
axles of clouds like dream cliffs.
Above that,

clear blue possibility.

Rising on thermals, like eagles
searching for higher winds,

soaring always

into the burning sun . . . dreams
like melting wax:

Icarus
falling upon rocks of the sea.

THE BLACK UNICORN

The clock hanging on my drawing room wall
never sounded so loud;
the eccentric ticking monotonously reminds me
of days of my life.

Ghosts share this silent house, their tiny sounds
personified by the noise of age and failing wood.
Floorboards moan with each step. I scrape
my feet along, mostly to hush the boards' screeching,

Listen, Spirit noise: a small ringing like shredded voices in
the hum of telephone wire, cloudy and distant.
These spirits chant mostly unintelligible stuff from the past.
Do you remember happier days? They whisper.
Star-crossed lovers once lived here.

My other self chimes in at the sound of the clock.
And we digress to endless possibilities.
I talk to myself, a sign of dementia,
but it's these damned voices that keep me remembering
the love I lost.

When I was a boy, I had a magic horse named Smoke,
a unicorn, black as the darkest thought.
Made of rags, he carried me away to magic lands.
Adrift we frolicked in the surf and sang songs of smoke,
the magic horse. It was a time of searching and finding,
of escape from pains of being too young or too old.
Growing up was not easy at my house.

For only a moment I looked away, and the house became a
   dreary refuge
without you, my old horse, skin glistening with sweat,
and hip bones showing. Teeth ground to nothing, eyes dull and
   sick . . .
Without you I am a sick eagle, grounded, and reaching for the sky,
and I am lonely.

The shrinks reckoned: dysfunctional home, make-believe,
dark, swimming dreams. When they asked me about the horse,
I told them everything, where every dream and nightmare
was buried . . . I still hear the voices.

IN A COUNTRY GRAVEYARD

Feeling is freedom in this peaceful afternoon of the dead.
Decoration Day in a country cemetery, a gaudy event.
We come with medallions of flowers
and trinkets to honor our dead,
a kind of floral fantasy.

Late afternoon stretches long shadows
across the lawn, peaceful,
this community of the dead.

A startling quietness pervades these mounds.
No longer molded in corporal frames,
soulless lumps of clay
in ragged rows, like a field of planted corn.

Still, a presence here
drifts up from the vaults through carpeted grass,
breathes the sense we are all the same,
all who come here
part of the great flow of energy into some universal heart
which beats collectively for us all.

The Cellist

Even though the case is cumbersome,
she drags it to the concert hall each evening.
Musicians often acquire instruments
much the same way dog owners resemble their pets.
In this case the image is not true.
The girl is skinny, and the cello is large.

The beauty of this instrument is exceptional,
Stradivarius, a priceless work of art
a melodious instrument capable of rich, dark enchantment.
Nothing surpasses the voluptuous sound.
Like music from heavenly choirs, the cello's guttural sound
resonates throughout the concert hall.

She holds her baritone lover
between wide-spread legs,
plays something from a string quartet by Laos Janacek.
Softly draws the bow over strings
pulling the dark, melancholy song filling the heart of the great hall.
Sweat runs down her back, hair wet on brow.
The sound comes up from the damp between her legs,
and a love song is born
in the night.

A Little Psalm

DREAM WALKING IN THE MIDNIGHT GARDEN

Walking in my garden at midnight
after the moon has settled above Walden's Ridge,
and stars cascade the sky.
Poems dripping from the horns of Taurus,
golden nuggets of light shooting through space,
transforming my mind to romantic butter.

Looking up feels small, insignificant,
the magnificent cosmic . . .
it could be a carnival for the lords of heaven.

Starry Night rushing headlong
through the immensity riding the juggernaut.

And when I lie in the dreaming hour,
stars will fill the sky, calling my name.

I Have in Mind a Garden of Bees

They come in hordes, the bees,
searching for a place to hive—
the carcass lying in the field might do,
the clover so vital to their work.

I watch as the small beast performs
his creative dance mapping exactly the
longitudes and latitudes
of the succulent clover or sourwood grove.
Little circular flights routing the way to the
honey pots.

The bees' low thrum resonates
the glade startled by spring's migration.
Burrowing deep in the bloated bull,
bees make the sound of a machine, mass
producing and efficient.
The ox comes alive with the sounds
they create.

The glade buzzes with activity.
The succulent savor of honey . . .
Wind on the backs of new leaves . . .

MESSAGE OF SNOW

Winter drops pale reminders
of dogwood blossoms,
wild cherry petals.

A snowy caul sculpts coffin
of fallen logs.

I cross the solitary trails of deer
in fields and along the wood line;
their hoof-dragged tracks declare
beauty not always a blessing.

Black crows glisten against silvered
tops of trees, seem worried their clay
feet may dissolve, consumed
in this brooding blizzard.
Even in this now-vacant orchard
of summer fruit, weeds
and thorns.

A capricious wind splits shards
of ice from pine boughs prickling
shrouded ground or nails through
the perfect hands of Christ. The bones
of pines ache. Their needles sieve sounds
like whispering voices.

Turning toward a small light
in the valley, the moon's white gaze
illuminates my half-hidden tracks.

There will be no darkness tonight.

The Barn We Built

Forty years ago we built the barn, you and I,
after the kids were asleep, until 3 and 4 a.m.
We were young and didn't care about time.
We worked nailing and sawing and making love
in our creation.
We were alone in the world, you and I ,
and in love. Nothing else mattered . . .

The old barn still stands like a monument in time.
Oh, if only we could build that barn again.

BURDENS

My troubles seemed small and far away.
I went to sleep in cool spring sun.
The day unrolled in corrugated rain on the lake,
causing the mallards to fly uncontrolled flights
across the meadow.

A Little Psalm

Walking east into East River
Thick muddy water covers my head
I go down where the fishes are
Walk in reeds and green kelp
People float at all levels
Eyes wide and fearsome
Honey-breath palms cover my mouth
They float over me
I can see the retracted hands

IMAGE IN THE LAKE

I saw my father walking by the lake.
All day he has sauntered in and out of my thoughts.

Once when I was fishing in Mud Creek,
I saw his image in the water, staring up
through the *Hydrilla verticillita* like a troll
under the bridge of my life.

I don't ever remember my father kissing me as a child.
I don't remember hate or emotion or harsh words.
Sometimes I would have welcomed harsh words,
any words. I wanted desperately to know him,
to make him proud.

But he kept his life to himself, and if he felt any
emotion, it was not obvious.
I think he only stayed with Mother because it was easier
to simply exist and take love someplace else.
We were merely objects in his life.

I never lived in a house filled with love,
yet there was always the perception of love,
the intent to love, the need, and I never knew it was missing
until years later. Years after I stopped trying to make him talk.

A SMALL ALLEGORY

. . . and behold a white horse!
           —Rev. 19:11

The red-tailed hawk calls to his own.
Crows respond with terrible threats.
Scenes of end times play out in my mind:
the hawk, the lion of the tribe of Judah.

No one knows how the end will come, maybe
a crash on Wall Street, ten thousand points
in a jangle of nerves. Maybe someone
will finally push the button, or maybe,
maybe the lion will simply appear.

The hawk ignores the crows and continues
his morning ritual. His mate responds faintly
somewhere at a distance. Knowing her
to be weaker, but faithful, the humble warrior
sails off into the dark woods to hunt and kill
for her. The crows plot how he might die.

Morning light, new light, filters
through summer trees, the birds' song
of revelation.

SOLDIER

Vietnam is the backyard of his mind, an ancient
enemy he still fights. They only come out at night
or during the rainy season; black faces
greasy with hate.

NV Regulars infest the woods beside the lake,
punji sticks and dark holes holding
deadly snakes. And the tunnels . . . he remembers
crawling the tunnels with nothing more than a .45
and guts. Cocaine and acid crawled into those tunnels.

Night awakens in a bed of sweat,
jungle rain, taste of gunpowder. Feet still sore
from fungus and the socks that rotted off
during weeks trampling rice fields.

Once he spoke of sleep that overtook him
in a bunker the VC had built and how
friendly fire blew him out of his cot.
Death so close no one breathed.

He lurches out of bed, belly flat on the floor,
waiting for a round to explode; sometimes the dreams so real,
he runs through the backyard screaming
at his stricken platoon.

But when the serum works, he is calm, almost normal.
In these times, you know he is at peace, or at least
the rage is under control. He has tried to be a good
father and husband. They know never to ask him
about the war.

NIGHT VISITORS

All week, emotions have been building. An abscess
of memory that won't heal. Forgiveness is not a
commodity that can be bargained. Walking familiar corridors,
the house becomes a ghost prison, my own little demi-gods
wanting something I can no longer give:
some calamitous event from which
there is no absolute truth, rude secrets that can't be told.
A moment of truth compels a greater bondage
than dozens of years of lies.

Sometimes the noise of whispers in the room is like
"Ancient Voices of Children" playing in a barnyard, some ancient game,
those far-distant voices from antiquity, all speaking at once,
as wind sieved through dry grass, believing truth, as innocent lambs
can be trusted. Rogue memories I keep, lucid recollections.
They line the walls, speak through yellowed photographs,
warn me what I am, what I might become. Plethora
of strange voices . . .

4:30 a.m.
George Crumb's timbral essay paying homage to Lorca and the
haunting
image of his poetry. As the children speak,
and, for the first time, shadows fade, and the voices
are silent.

*Note: George Crumb is a contemporary composer from Charleston,
West Virginia. This poem references his song cycle, "Ancient Voices of
Children," based on texts by Federico Garcia Lorca.*

WINTER SUN

The fact that light is leaving,
something in the winter sun,
the angle it strikes my eyes,
the more than usual thin, pale light,
or the way fields lie in the thinner
light of midday, makes me sad.
Something about the equinox
I don't understand.

Maybe the way the sun lies on hillsides
in small patches of gold light
or filters itself through
tall sage making a red-brown glow
you can almost smell.

Mostly the sadness comes in me
from somewhere I can only feel,
a hollow thought
after the light has done its work.

I lament the heaviness of the winter sun
as it falls through the glass
onto the floor at my feet.

I lament the frozen wind that searches
continually through skeleton trees
against cold horizons
for some logic for the changing of light.

I lament the passing of light, the gradual
ebbing of day to a glimmer sunset,
the subtle metamorphosis toward early sleep.

FLYING LIKE ANGELS

We made John's Place an icon,
Pabst Blue Ribbon like sacred wine,
a watering hole for the lost.
Somehow we always got back to school.

Minds blew at the edge of knowledge,
psychedelic dynamo, free-love time,
leaning toward darkness or light
—freedom hard.

José Garcia wore ringlets of love
in army green, stepped on a landmine,
came home in a box.
Didn't make it back to school.

We thought smoke-filled days, liquid nights
would never end. Now it seems like,
what's the song? Purple Haze . . .
But we were cool in that purple mist,

driving the dark side of the road,
flying like angels going nowhere
in a blue-flowered yellow van
and the red door painted black.

PASSING BY PLEASANT HILL BAPTIST CHURCH AT DUSK

A sinner in a Ford truck sucking on Pabst Blue Ribbon
half-drunk, not half in love with anything,
I wonder what the Lord must think.

Tires rip and crack the graveled road,
offer jolted prayer on my behalf
to a God who does not entirely believe in me.
I don't even know what prayer really is:

cicada's choiring through pines,
an owl's hoot over a shadowed lake,
or me stranded on uncertain knees
to beg forgiveness of sins I don't even remember.

My old truck brakes at the ramp.
I stand upright in my spirit, wholly lighted,
baptized in moonlight,
slide a john boat into the dark waters of absolution . . .
The only salvation I may ever know.

SOLITARY PLACES

How often I think of you
a finger of smoke moving through my wooded heart
gone to earth
        the deep earth . . .
I, nothing more than quick hands moving the black dirt
        with roses and recollections

WORKING AT THE CANNERY

Once, I worked at a cannery hopeless as O'Neill's Hairy Ape.
Mostly high school dropouts, low incomes trying to survive
the brutal life of phobias.
I worked the subculture, third shift clean-up crew.

Buck was a lead man, a joke management played,
savior to the clean-up crew,
a collective for their hang-ups,
their sins.
All aggression ended at his door.
He forgave each trespass.

Buck feared frogs, something about the eyes.
Even so, we chased him spitefully, knowing it hurt.
No one cared for his nightmare.

Once he climbed to the roof of a loading dock, jumped
on a boxcar to avoid
cold, warty skin.

He cried,
begged,
pleaded,
pissed his pants;
we laughed.

Descending into that peculiar eccentricity,
my greatest fear was I'd be like them.
Then, the fact: I was.

AT THE BATTERY STORE ON EAST MAIN

Leaning on the store front,
awaiting morning handouts,
he said he'd been to Viet Nam.
Asked if I had been,
for some reason I said yes, and
I was here to buy a battery.

He called me Sir, the way he'd been raised.
I hated that humility, regretted my lie.

Said in Cambodia he had a mama-san, all the beer he wanted,
saw some bad shit.
I said I'd seen some bad shit.
He said, *I killed women and children . . . and dogs.*
Asked me, did I have any chickens?
He had lotsa chickens
at home, grew up on a farm down around Macon.

Said the voices wouldn't let him *be*—
everywhere the damn voices.
Then, the serum that made his eyes
thick and pale.

Void

The lunatic's in the hall
   —Pink Floyd

I need to say some important thing tonight,
to release some insight that might seem right,
to say this thought above all thought is what you need . . .
But I have nothing to say, nothing bleeps in my head,
no giant cosmic idea lurks in the key strokes to satisfy
this awful yearning. It may be a song without sound.

I was thinking of knives and forks in the kitchen drawer,
how they must wish for the light, to be sunk into a pork chop
and rammed into the hollow of mouths. Or the sink and
its constant . . . drip . . . drip . . . drip . . .

I thought of night closing around me like a womb
where water has broken and the dry dust of my typewriter
is all I have to breathe. I bang the keys hoping for some
relief from this drought. My eyes are heavy, sleep evasive,
always. It's down the hall. Just in the next room.
Always where I am not. I have nothing to say tonight.

The lunatic's in the yard and in the hall and the stranger's
in my head looking out blistered eyes; sleep looks at me.
The lunatic's in the yard and in the hall . . .

I thought of the hot plate that could warm my hands as well as
my soup. I thought of the barrier between me and the ones I love.
I thought of the dissonance of life and my life. I have nothing to say.
The dark side of the moon is where I am.
My shadow appears down the hall, watching as I scrape along
through the reality of empty beds and the heartless arms of lovers
knowing, as I know, that no one is here to save me. Like Kafka,
I morph into the lunatic I have created.
Into darkness. The mad-dog night is all that keeps me company.
Bent dreams wait for me and the sleep I am promised.

WORKING IN THE ASYLUM

Once I worked in a mental institution. People out of touch
with themselves. The inmates are in their own world and generally
don't bother anyone.

Nothing I've witnessed matches the sadness in their faces

I was on duty as a male nurse on a cold winter night in January
and heard a scream, or what sounded like a scream.
The halls were cold and dim. The inmates were in bed, or should
have been.

I walked out in the hall, saw a light from a doorway. I started
toward the light, and I saw a shadow move along the wall.
This is getting pretty spooky, I thought. Something about crazy people.
Just at that moment another scream. I rushed down the hall.
   There was
a silver-haired black lady who must have been 80 years old, cold
   and crying.
She took me by the arm, looking through wet eyes, and said:
I'll call you my son. He's supposed to come and get me.
I don't think I'm ever going to get home. I got her back in her room
   and
helped her back into bed. She touched my face
and said, *can I touch your face?* All the while her hand was against
my face, I thought I felt something like a mild shock or perhaps
something tingly like a cell phone on buzz. She had the strangest
   eyes,

deep black almost. You couldn't see the pupils. *I'm going to pray for you, mister,*
before I die. She didn't really look at me when she spoke. She stared past me to
someplace that only she knew. *You're a good man,* she absently repeated. *You are a*
good man, I'm going to pray for you before I die. You're a good . . .

Her hand slid slowly down my face. I put her arm under the cover and left
her resting comfortably. I felt different, like some important thing had
happened in my life. I don't know, like maybe an out-of-body experience.
Did it really happen, and did I feel a shock? The whole thing was so unearthly.
Maybe I drank too much coffee? It was cold that night. Or maybe she was an
angel, passing on a message I need to know but haven't yet realized.

Prozac Dream

I don't know, I said when she asked me
to describe the feeling. A dark room,
maybe, dread of the next few
minutes . . . not happy for no reason.
With Prozac and Paxil,
the monsters hid in tremors, bad
dreams, night sweats. For a while.
But then, I don't know,
something I meant to do got left out,
like when you see a gray sheet
of rain slanting across a field,
the blind white eye of some lost animal
seeking shelter. She said, you keep on going.
I said, there is no air in this place.
The walker in white helmet and suit
slips away like dust in the stillness of space.
In perfect calm, he drifts away.
The slow hand of a lover
waves from behind a window, hesitantly,
to someone leaving in rain.
Someone who is always leaving.
Nothing changes.
The tightness of space preserves everything.

SHOOTING BOTTLES IN THE TENNESSEE RIVER

Our headlights bounced
across Swafford bottoms,
the old, rusted out, '47 Chevy truck
struggling through two inches
of rain and eight inches of mud,
groaning to satisfy our lust.
We had tied one on and
we were ready to kill something,
anything, eyes in the headlights,
a deer, a fox . . .

I remember we stuck the truck
at the Red Barn and waded through
fog and drizzle for a half mile
to the river. Brains soaked
with alcohol and rain, we
threw bottles in the water and
shot at what we could see
with the dim flashlight.

Most of the bottles
bobbed out of sight,
pulled into the darker
edges of light by the
muddy river, floated
off into the night
where we were headed.

www.ingramcontent.com/pod-product-compliance
Lightning Source LLC
Chambersburg PA
CBHW032022090426
42741CB00006B/703